This book belongs to

....

About Katha

Katha, a nonprofit organisation working with and in story and storytelling since 1988, is one of India's top publishing houses. Katha's main focus is on introducing an array of writings from the many oral and written traditions of India to children, ages 0-17. Classy productions, child-friendly layouts and superb illustrations go in tandem with excellent writing. Katha works with a growing pool of writers, translators and literary enthusiasts. Our constant striving is for greater reach and impact amongst teachers and students, policy makers and the corporate sector.

Our mission: To enhance the joys of reading. To help every child realise his/her potential through community enriching, quality learning so that no child lives in poverty. To help break down gender, social, cultural and economic stereotypes through story and storytelling. And to enhance the role of translation as a counter-divisive tool in nation building.

Our belief: Stories help create friendships of a rare kind to culturelink people, faiths and creative impulses. Stories are the life-savers of future nations.

Our credo: Uncommon creativities for a common good.

KATHA

Geeta Dharmarajan | Art by Sonal Panse

a jungle safari

KATHA

Geeta Dharmarajan | Art by Sonal Panse

a jungle safari

Shhh! You are inside the Mudumalai forest, in the hump-backed hills of the Western Ghats in South India. In it live elephants and giant flying squirrels, spotted deer and sambars, jackals and hyenas, bears and birds, and ...

"TIGERS," said the man, who helped you climb on to Bhama's back, an hour ago.

He said, "Just yesterday, my daughter and I were frightened by a humungous tiger that jumped into our path. Luckily we were on the elephant," he went on. "Same one that you are on now, Bhama. If not for her, we would be inside the tiger's stomach now. Food for a week!"

You had smiled, thinking, How nice if I could spot a tiger!

"Anyone can see a tiger," says Gopan, your mahout. "If you're lucky, you will see a gaur, the Indian bison!"

Bison? Who wants to see a bison? Which is just another ox. Okay, so it is the largest of the bovines. Its muscles ripple more than an ordinary bull's. And it is bigger than the true bison of America and Europe. So what?

He said, "Just yesterday, my daughter and I were frightened by a humungous tiger that jumped into our path. Luckily we were on the elephant," he went on. "Same one that you are on now, Bhama. If not for her, we would be inside the tiger's stomach now. Food for a week!"

You had smiled, thinking, How nice if I could spot a tiger!

"Anyone can see a tiger," says Gopan, your mahout. "If you're lucky, you will see a gaur, the Indian bison!"

Bison? Who wants to see a bison? Which is just another ox. Okay, so it is the largest of the bovines. Its muscles ripple more than an ordinary bull's. And it is bigger than the true bison of America and Europe. So what?

You want to see a tiger!

"Hath! Hath!" Gopan calls out. It is the command for Bhama to move!

Now you are swaying through filtered sunlight, through the overpowering smell of lantana, on Bhama's broad back.

Bhama is a big, tame mother elephant with large tattered ears. Her domed head is prickly with coarse hair. If you sat on her without the metal seats draped in old cloth, her hairs would jab you, you think.

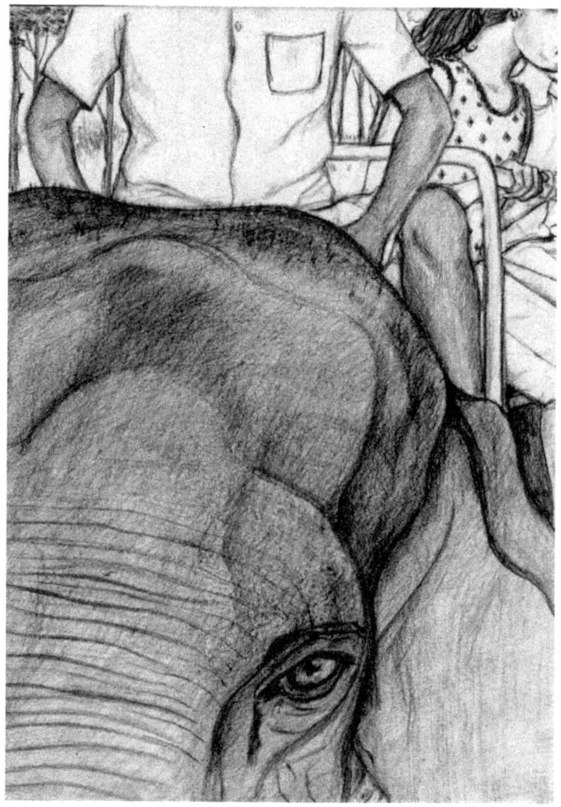

A sambar twitches its left ear at you from a thicket.

You see fluttering yellow butterflies, pale as a winter sunbeam.

A Malabar giant squirrel waves its red-brown tail, flying from tree to tree in a sweeping arc.

You see a rock.

"Rock," laughs Gopan, softly. "That's the camouflaging greyness of an elephant."

"W...wild?"

Gopan nods.

"He's in musth," he whispers.

A sambar twitches its left ear at you from a thicket.

You see fluttering yellow butterflies, pale as a winter sunbeam.

A Malabar giant squirrel waves its red-brown tail, flying from tree to tree in a sweeping arc.

You see a rock.

"Rock," laughs Gopan, softly. "That's the camouflaging greyness of an elephant."

"W...wild?"

Gopan nods.

"He's in musth," he whispers.

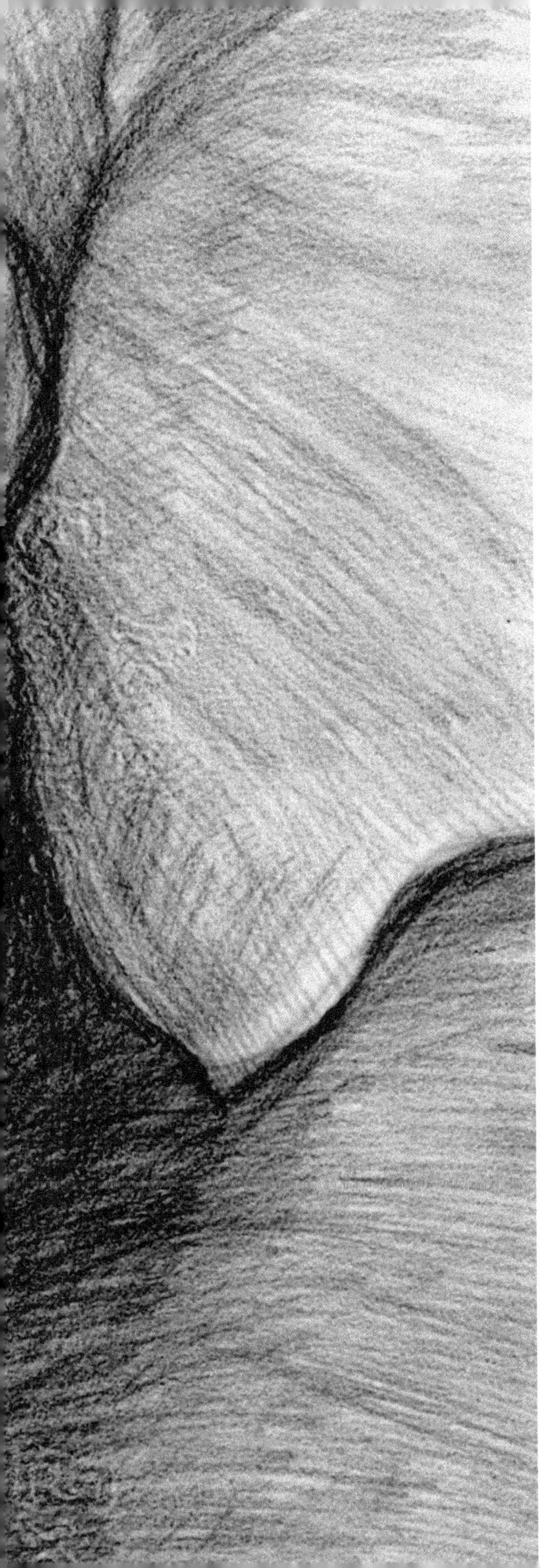

The massive head turns in your direction. Wetness oozes from near the tusker's eyes. He looks angry. He's very close. How did you think he was a rock?

Your heart hammers against your ribcage. Gopan senses your fear.

"It's okay," he says, half-turning around. His eyes smile.

"There's a ravine between us."

"And brave Bhama! She'll keep us safe."

"Hala! Hala!" Gopan calls.

Wind ruffles the tops of white ghostly trees.

You leave the beaten path and move into the undergrowth, beneath teak trees in flower.

Bhama snorts. She stops. Raising her foot she feels under it with her trunk that can lift anything from a tiny pin to a log of wood. Is there a thorn in her right foot?

Gopan, whose hair stands on end ever since, "... one moonlit night I could have been killed by a bear but wasn't, thanks to Bhama," mutters something to her. She bends her knee for him. He slides on to it, then jumps to the ground. Then he disappears. Where to?

Bhama shifts from one leg to another. When you look sideways and down, you can see she is chewing away. She sends her boneless trunk out for more grass. Placid.

Sitting on top of her you feel almost as peaceful, despite the shadows shifting in the trees.

Then ...

"Bison!" whispers Gopan, scurrying back on his short bow-legs. "Gaur!" He is pointing to some tracks that you can hardly see.

"Hala! Hala!"

Atop Bhama again, with his left foot he guides her in a northwesterly direction into Mudumalai's long twilight on the elusive trail of the gaur!

Bhama seems to catch the excitement in the air. She shuffles through the undergrowth, trampling down white wild mushrooms that glimmer in the sun, her massive head cutting across shimmering spider webs that stretch across your path. Coolness descends.

You come to a bog of black mud that looks as if it has been trampled by many hooves. Gopan circles it. And ...

"Gaur," he mutters, certain.

"Hath!"

You move again. In a forest, it isn't the seeing that's important, you decide. It's the expecting to see that's exciting! And then ... you see it!

One single bison, big, strong, imposing! Little insects milling around his dark wet eyes, his feet slightly splayed apart, his flat jutting-out horns catching the last soft rays of the sun, trickling in through the leaves. Shadows dance on his dark skin.

Huge. Absolutely enormous. You realize you are holding your breath. You look at the bison.

The bison looks at you.

And what's between? Nothing but scrub. A straggly lantana or two. Fear! He must be ten feet tall, you mutter, though Gopan has told you gaurs are rarely ever more than seven feet at the shoulder.

He's massive. He looks lost somehow. In need of a friend. You stand and stare at each other for a few frozen seconds.

Then he is just a rustle in the undergrowth. Once you see a flash of his yellow-brown head. Once, his white-stockinged feet in the whispering undergrowth. You already think of him as a friend. A strange combination of fear and excitement gnaws at your insides.

Bhama gives glorious chase. The roar of a distant tiger does not scare her. She is not afraid of the pandemonium in the sky as monkeys leap hither and thither. She is not scared by the darkness that comes down like buckets of black paint hurled in your direction.

Because of her you venture through the dense dark forest, expecting the tiger to appear. NOW! Worrying that the tusker is surely charging at you from behind, wondering if the bear that attacked Gopan is planning a guerrilla attack, peering into the gloom of sunset, then ...

Sighting one gaur ... one more!

“A family,” says Gopan, his wheezy voice, low and almost indistinct. “You have brought your luck with you today,” he says, grinning at you, flashing broken teeth.

You grin back. You bend. Touch fingertips to Bhama’s side. Who is, of course, chomping away. You are ready to leave the darkening, threatening forest, and get back to civilization.

You hit the main road where a lorry chugs on the spot, like an athlete doing a stationary jog, and Bhama who had not been scared of a tiger, a big burly bear or muscle-rippling bisons, now stops, frozen, as if paralyzed!

Bhama shifts her weight uncomfortably from foot to foot and waits for the lorry to go away.

... Scared baby!

Fascinating Facts on Mudumalai and the Gaur

Aren't you eager to visit the Mudumalai forest? To see the gaur, the elephant, the tiger and the birds? But how much do we know about this reserve and its magnificent wildlife?

The Indian wildlife sanctuaries and natural parks are homes to many of our wild animals – the majestic tiger, the graceful elephant, the magnificent peacock and the gigantic rhinoceros! These sanctuaries and parks spread across the country also offer a fascinating variety of flora and fauna. Do you know that India has around 441 wildlife sanctuaries and some 80 national parks?

The famous Mudumalai wildlife sanctuary is situated at a height of 1,000 metres in the Nilgiri Hills in the Western Ghats of Tamil Nadu. "Mudumalai" means ancient hills! The total reserve area is about 321 square metres. And the Mysore-Ooty highway with its scenic views runs through it.

Nature has been lavish in giving the sanctuary thickly wooded hills, plateaus, deep valleys, waterfalls, rivers, marshes and streams. It is a varied mix of flatlands, undulating parklands and open grasslands. You will find both dense, mixed and moist deciduous forests. Bamboos, natural teak and blooming trees are some of the flora found here.

The fauna is fascinatingly varied. Elephants, gaurs, common langurs, tigers, leopards, chitals, panthers, sloth bears, pythons, four-horned antelopes, otters, crocodiles, giant flying squirrels, sambars, hyenas, wild boars, spotted deer, jackals, porcupines and more – they all have their homes at Mudumalai!

There are lots of birds too – peacocks, red spur fowls, grey partridge quails, Malabar whistling thrushes, large racket-tailed dronges, magpies, robins, spotted babblers, green pigeons, brown doves, Malabar grey hornbills, bulbuls, mynas, eagles, hawks, buzzards, falcons and king vultures – besides some migratory water birds!

The best season to visit the sanctuary is during March-June.

Gaur: The Indian Bison

Many of us know very little about the tallest and the most splendid specimens of wild oxen in the world – the Indian bison, or the gaur. Few other animals can match its rustic charm and muscled power! The gaur can be seen in the wild in the forests of southern and eastern India, Burma, Thailand, Malaysia, Cambodia, Laos, Vietnam, Nepal and Bhutan! One can easily spot a bull or calf running alongside its mother or a large herd grazing in the jungles.

Here are some incredible facts about the gaur:

The gaur is a large animal. Male gaurs are black in colour, while female gaurs are brown.The hides of both the male and the female are white below the knee of each leg, making it appear as if they are wearing white stockings! Gaur calves, on the other hand, are light brown in colour. Adult gaur bulls can grow up to two metres tall and weigh between 650 and 1,000 kilograms. The females are smaller in size.

The gaur lives in grassy clearings and in evergreen and deciduous forests. It can even live in altitudes up to 1,800 metres! In North East India, one finds the tamer version of the gaur, the mithun! And the barasingha, or the twelve-horned gaur is found in the forested areas of Karnataka and Assam.

Gaurs are herbivores. They feed mainly on grass. During times of drought, they may eat leaves, creepers and plants. Gaurs usually spend the night in a forest and emerge into open grassy lands or clearings to feed during the day. They feed in the morning, rest in the afternoon, feed some more in the evening and return to the forest cover at night.

Gaurs live in herds of around 10, however, herds of up to 40 too, have been seen. An adult male bull leads the herd. The bulls may fight amongst themselves to establish dominance over a herd. Male bulls may also live in bachelor herds. Gaurs sound calls to warn the herd of danger and also to communicate among themselves. Licking one another is another means of bonding among them!

The sad fact is that today, gaurs are endangered. They are beginning to be seen more in protected sanctuaries around India. Their numbers are becoming less and less, day by day, as human encroachment and cattle diseases fast reduce their habitat and population across India. Let us act now and save this wonderful creature!

For more information, you could contact any of the wildlife protection societies based in India and abroad.

Geeta Dharmarajan founded Katha in 1988, with a children's magazine called *Tamasha!*. Her deep interest in social work in education led to the development of a special story-based pedagogy and curriculum for children coming from underserved communities. She views stories as a means of fostering unity by reinforcing diversity. Previously, she was one of the editors of *The Pennsylvania Gazette*, the magazine of the Ivy League University of Pennsylvania, and *Target*, a magazine for children which marked the beginning of her 31 years of professional editorial experience. She has 31 books and over 400 published pieces to her credit.

Sonal Panse is a freelance artist and writer based in Nashik in Maharashtra. She does realistic, imaginative and abstract artwork in a variety of media, and has written several articles on a range of subjects. Her work has been featured in print and web publications in India, Australia and the United States. Sonal has also exhibited her paintings in London and Mumbai, and is currently working on a novel.

KATHA

First published © Katha, 2005

ISBN 978-81-89020-69-9

KATHA is a registered nonprofit devoted to enhancing the joys of reading amongst children and adults. Katha Schools are situated in the slums and streets of Delhi and tribal villages of Arunachal Pradesh.
A3 Sarvodaya Enclave, Sri Aurobindo Marg
New Delhi 110 017
Phone: 4141 6600 . 4182 9998 . 2652 1752
Fax: 2651 4373
E-mail: marketing@katha.org, Website: www.katha.org

Ten per cent of sales proceeds from this book will support the quality education of children studying in Katha Schools.
Katha regularly plants trees to replace the wood used in the making of its books.

stories in translation

Satyadas

Bimal Kar | Art by Neeta Gangopadhya

A story about truth and honesty compromised when material well-being arrives. The story showcases with sensitivity the exit of humane values with the advent of material wealth and prosperity.

While the charcoal sketches bring to life the humble life and household of Raghunath, the story, originally written in Bengali, is about the decline in human values as one falls a prey to greed. As the prologue to the book describes, it is a story "exploring truth, falsehood and everything in between." — The Hindu

A stranger with an unkempt look walks up to the grocery shop of Raghunath on a bleak afternoon of ceaseless drizzle. "You can call me Satyadas", he says, and he will make Raghunath, as well as the readers, rediscover certain painful truths about human nature. Illustrated by Neeta Gangopadhya, this slim book is a must-read for the young and the old alike. — The Telegraph

The Myna from Peacock Garden

Naiyer Masud | Art by Premola Ghose

Work is on in full swing at the Royal Peacock Garden to install a Wondrous Cage that will house forty talking hill mynas. Soon, the Cage and its lively, twittering occupants are entrusted to Kale Khan's care. But he steals a myna for his little motherless daughter, who has long been asking him for one. What lies in store for Kale Khan ... and the beautiful historic city of Lucknow?

The dreamlike quality and the meticulous attention to language make Masud's writing so delightfully different.
— Mehraab

...[a] masterful portrayal of the Lucknow of yore.
— The World of Urdu Poetry

www.ingramcontent.com/pod-product-compliance
Ingram Content Group UK Ltd.
Pitfield, Milton Keynes, MK11 3LW, UK
UKHW061307190726
13845UKWH00039B/1277

9 788189 020392